DIVINE
ESSENCE

Books by John-Roger

Awakening Into Light
Baraka
Blessings of Light
Buddha Consciousness
The Christ Within & The Disciples of Christ
with the Cosmic Christ Calendar
The Consciousness of Soul
A Consciousness of Wealth
Divine Essence
Dream Voyages
Drugs
Dynamics of the Lower Self
Forgiveness: The Key to the Kingdom
God Is Your Partner
Inner Worlds of Meditation
The Journey of a Soul
Loving…Each Day
Manual on Using the Light
The Master Chohans of the Color Rays
Passage Into Spirit
The Path to Mastership
Possessions, Projections & Entities
The Power Within You
Psychic Protection
Q & A Journal from the Heart
Relationships — Love, Marriage and Spirit
Sex, Spirit & You
The Signs of the Times
The Sound Current
The Spiritual Family
The Spiritual Promise
Spiritual Warrior
The Tao of Spirit
Walking with the Lord
The Way Out Book
Wealth & Higher Consciousness

For further information, Please contact:
MSIA®
P.O. Box 513935
Los Angeles, CA 90051-1935
323/737-4055
soul@msia.org   www.msia.org

DIVINE ESSENCE

(*Baraka*)

JOHN-ROGER

MANDEVILLE PRESS
Los Angeles, California

Mandeville Press

P.O. Box 513935

Los Angeles, California 90051-1935

e-mail: jrbooks@msia.org

Visit us on the Web at www.mandevillepress.org

I.S.B.N. 1-893020-04-5

CONTENTS

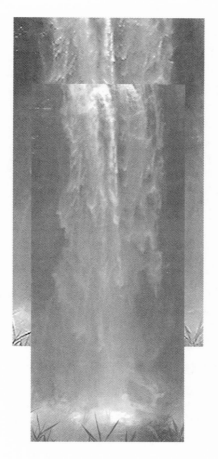

INTRODUCTION

JOHN-ROGER

THE FORCE THAT IS THE SUPREME LORD
OF ALL UNIVERSES IS SO OMNIPOTENT AND
SO FAR BEYOND WHAT THE HUMAN MIND
CAN ENVISION THAT THERE ARE NO WORDS
THAT CAN DESCRIBE OR GIVE SENSE TO IT.
SINCE LANGUAGE IS A PRIMARY FORM OF
COMMUNICATION, HOWEVER,
WE USE WORDS AS REFERENCE POINTS
THAT HAVE MEANING TO MOST OF US.

WE ARE ALL spiritual beings.

We are all of God.

We are all of Spirit.

There is nothing that is not of God.

There is no one who is not of Spirit.

JOHN-ROGER

THE SPARK OF GOD individualized within each human being is the Soul. That is the basic element of our existence. The Soul is forever connected to God, perfectly and intimately. It is the source from which we draw our life.

Introduction

THE NATURE AND THE ESSENCE of the Soul are joy. The Soul is joyful because it is of God and knows it.

JOHN-ROGER

THE HUMAN CONSCIOUSNESS is somewhat different. It is made up of elements other than the Soul and these elements—the body, imagination, emotions, mind, subconscious, and unconscious—can cloud the clarity of spiritual vision and interfere with our ability to perceive Spirit directly.

Introduction

THE INNER ELEMENTS of human consciousness, most of which are invisible, are actually microcosms of greater, outer levels of existence. Within each of us is a rich world of feelings, imagination, thoughts, etc. We could spend an endless amount of time exploring these inner realities. And yet, they are only a reflection in miniature of what lies outside of our own consciousness. The beginning of the film "Contact" is a great visual for what I'm describing. You see seemingly infinite worlds and universes, which slowly reveal themselves to be within the eye of a young girl.

JOHN-ROGER

SOME REALMS, BOTH WITHIN US AND AROUND US, are of a positive nature, and others are of a negative nature. Not "good" and "bad," which is how we tend to categorize things, but like the positive and negative polarities of a battery. The two together create movement and action, the dynamics of life. One is a more inward pull, the other a more outward movement.

INTRODUCTION

THE PHYSICAL WORLD is one small part of our outer reality. The imagination and other levels of consciousness are not so obvious, yet we know them. Our physical body lives and moves in the physical world. Here we have experiences, from which we hopefully learn and grow. The human consciousness is intricate, however, and also exists on many other levels. The physical world and all our levels of consciousness, including the mind, emotions, imagination and unconscious, are only ten percent of our total existence.

FOR EVERY LEVEL WITHIN US, there is an outer level through which we can experience our creations—and eventually learn and grow. Our inner, personal imagination works in the "astral" realm outside of us where we give reality to our fantasies and imaginary scenes, often creating our own "monsters," illusions and delusions until we realize that there are better ways to guide our imagination.

The causal plane of existence reflects to us the emotional quality of our consciousness. On this level, we can experience our emotional creations and their power.

The mental realm corresponds to the mind, with all its confusions and doubts as well as its clarity and dynamic thrust.

The etheric realm is the area where the power of our subconscious and unconscious manifests. This is often where we store "incompletes," things that we do not want to handle and put into the "back of our minds." They don't go away, as we might hope. They surface, usually in unpredictable ways and timing, giving us the opportunity to face and complete what we have started.

ALL OF THESE LEVELS, as intricate and demanding as they can be, are only a small part of our consciousness. They are the "negative" pole of the battery. Their influence and power is designed to keep us closely involved with them.

THE SOUL is positive in nature. The realm of the Soul and the realms of Spirit above the Soul are designed to lift us and bring us freedom. In the positive realms, the lower worlds lose their influence. The plan and purpose of the lower worlds becomes clear and in that clarity is freedom.

Introduction

As an analogy of how the negative worlds function, suppose you are walking on a path in the mountains, and home is about ten miles away. You set off on your journey, feeling good. Everything seems fine. Then you come to an area where the terrain gets rough. Trees are down across the path, and it's muddy, rocky, and steep. Fog rolls in and it starts raining. You're having a hard time finding the trail. As you look for a way through, you scrape your leg or turn your ankle. Your physical body gets cold and your muscles start aching. You feel tired and lose your enthusiasm for this journey.

IN YOUR IMAGINATION, you start seeing the possibility that the entire ten miles is going to be like this. You start creating the image that it's never going to get any better, and you don't know how you'll ever make it home. Your emotions start reacting to this imaginary scene, and you start feeling discouraged and depressed. When you come to one more big tree down across your path and you can't find an easy way around it, you may start to cry.

THEN YOUR MIND COMES INTO PLAY and, based on what you've created in your imagination, it starts you thinking that maybe there's another way to get home; maybe if you go in another direction entirely, you'll find your way. You follow this new "direction" and turn away from the path that leads home.

THE UNCONSCIOUS LEVEL takes in all the information from your mind, emotions, and imagination, but doesn't have any tools to express on those levels. It just stores the information and then feeds it back to you, so that every new turn in the path becomes an aspect of the last turn, and all sorts of vague fears and illusions surface in your consciousness. They frighten and confuse you and prevent you from seeing clearly what is really present for you in each moment of your journey.

ALL OF THESE ASPECTS PLAY BACK AND FORTH in your consciousness, often so rapidly that you aren't aware of what you're doing inside yourself. You find yourself lost, sidetracked, confused and frightened as you move through your experience, trying to find your way home.

WHEN YOU CAN REACH BEYOND all these negative levels and perceive from the Soul, from the positive aspect of yourself, you can lift up in consciousness, see where your home is and see which path will lead you there. And whether the rough terrain lasts for ten miles or only a half mile, you can see what to do to traverse the path.

AT THAT POINT, you can go back into your journey and use all the levels of your consciousness as tools to your advantage. You can use your body to move you along the path toward your goal, your imagination to create the image of safely reaching home, and your emotions to keep you happy and joyful. You use your mind to decide on a good direction and keep you focused on completing that direction. And you use the areas of the unconscious to strengthen you as you learn to discern reality from illusion.

Guides and Wayshowers

INTO THIS MATRIX of positive and negative levels come those who are enlightened, who have discovered how these different levels work and fit together, and who have experienced the Soul and Spirit directly. We call them the masters and great teachers of humanity. They assist people to awaken to their greater destiny; they teach of God's love and God's plan.

LIVING IN THE HIGHER REALMS OF LIGHT, these great masters and teachers become imbued with the positive energy of Spirit. As they come into the lower worlds, they bring that energy with them.

The Soul within each person intuitively recognizes that energy from Spirit as its greater reality and moves toward it. When the Soul starts turning toward its true home, the grip of the lower levels is loosened and falls away. As we attune to our Soul, we learn and grow in our awareness of God and are finally able to transcend the lower levels of consciousness and reach our home in Spirit.

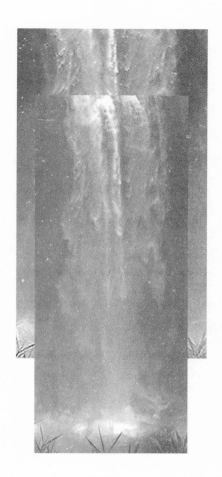

I

DIVINE PRESENCE

JOHN-ROGER

SPIRIT IS THE FORCE THAT GIVES YOU YOUR
LIFE, ENERGY, AND POWER. IT'S THAT SPARK OF
THE DIVINE THAT IS THE SOURCE OF YOUR
"GODNESS" OR GOODNESS.

THERE ARE INFINITE levels of consciousness and dimensions of space and time within a multitude of universes. This planet Earth is in only one of the many realms of Light. All consciousness, on all realms of Light including earth, is part of a greater order and plan of spiritual evolvement.

THE SPIRITUAL CONSCIOUSNESS of humanity extends through all realms, reaching from its home in the Soul realm down to the physical realm. In that sense, it exists on all realms simultaneously. Your awareness of one realm may be greater than of others, however, depending on the evolvement of your individual consciousness.

MOST PEOPLE have a greater awareness of this physical earth and of the imagination, emotions, mind and subconscious, and very little or no awareness of the higher realms of the Soul and Spirit.

There are people whose consciousness is more highly developed, however. They are aware not only of this physical world, but also of the higher realms of Spirit. These people are the great teachers, gurus and masters who come forward to teach and show the way to those who are ready to walk the spiritual path.

THERE ARE GREAT MASTERS who come from the lower realms of Light. Their message can be uplifting and inspiring; the abilities they demonstrate can be miraculous.

Some masters are connected to a universal consciousness from the high, positive realms of pure Spirit. They are aware of all the levels of consciousness, and they have the ability to work with, teach, guide, and show the way "home" to those Souls who are ready to lift out of the cycle of the lower levels and return to the Soul realm.

JESUS THE CHRIST was such a Master. Because he was so powerful and his impact on the Western world so great, people in Western culture usually relate to the Christ or the Christ consciousness as a manifestation of this higher level of spirit. Jews and Christians alike share in this tradition, for though Jews don't recognize Jesus as the Messiah, the concept of the Messiah is a very important part of their tradition.

Tʜᴇ Cʜʀɪsᴛ is a universal consciousness that dwells within everyone, although some people are more awakened to and aware of it than others. The teachings of the Christ (not a church interpretation of Jesus' teachings, but the message He brought) are universal. They don't conflict with any other teachings; they encompass all other teachings through their universal approach.

The consciousness of the Christ is the consciousness of pure Spirit. It exists within each one of us through the Soul.

The individual Soul of man exists as the indwelling Christ. Because most people are imperfectly aware of the Christ within, there is always at least one person on the planet who manifests the Christ. They demonstrate this higher consciousness so that others can see and recognize it.

THE CHRIST within one person can awaken the Christ within others. When you perceive the Christ consciousness, you begin to awaken to that greater expression in yourself.

THERE IS A LINE of spiritual masters called "Mystical Travelers" who work directly through the line of the Christ. In other places where the Christ is not the focus of universal spiritual force, this line of spiritual masters comes through the All, the It of Itself, or the Supreme God for which there is no name. The Mystical Traveler consciousness, as an agent of God, draws its energy from the pure, spiritual realms.

THE VALUE OF THE MYSTICAL TRAVELER is that it has traversed the realms of Light, extended itself into the physical form, and now uses the physical form to bring you the teachings on a verbal level. It explains to you that there is more to your existence than your body, mind, or emotions, that you are more than your physical expression.

THE MYSTICAL TRAVELER also has the ability to reach into the inner consciousness and strengthen your awareness of Soul until you start to feel that movement inside of you. When you sense that something's going on, you may run to the nearest book to read what it could be. The book won't give you the experience, though if it's by someone who knows what's going on, you can use it to clarify what your experience has been. Whatever you read, you must check the information out for yourself, in your own way, in the integrity of your own beingness.

THOSE WHO HAVE HELD the keys to the Mystical
Traveler Consciousness in the past have brought to
humanity the message of love, harmony, balance,
honesty and integrity. These spiritual messages have
sometimes been given directly and openly, in a public
way. At other times, the Mystical Travelers live private
lives, quietly holding the spiritual energy like an
anchor from Spirit into this world.

Some historical figures who have held the keys to
the Traveler consciousness are Rama, Eli Hu, and
Jesus the Christ. Someone is always holding the keys
to this consciousness, though they don't always work
openly with people. A great deal of the Traveler's
work is done silently, in the inner consciousness.

LOOK AT THE MESSAGE of each one of these Travelers of Light and Sound and you'll see that the message is always the same. The messengers who bear the Light and Sound bring forward the same message time and again, because people continue to either forget or corrupt it.

ONLY A FEW PEOPLE stand out as pinnacles of this Light force, letting themselves be used as transformers to step down the high spiritual energy so that it can be used in this world. Each person who is divinely endowed with this knowledge comes to restate the ancient message, bring forward a particular dispensation for that time, and place it within the consciousness of humanity. This is the spiritual glory to which we are all heirs.

THE UNIVERSAL MESSAGE of Spirit is again being presented. Two thousand years ago, Jesus said, "He that believeth in Me, the works that I do shall he do also; and even greater works than these shall he do; because I go unto my Father." (John 14:12) What was this message? Was he speaking of His physical form? No, He was speaking from the spiritual consciousness. He was speaking from the Christ consciousness when He said, "I am the Alpha and the Omega." (Revelations 1:8) That's the Christ Spirit that is in all of us.

MUHAMMAD GAVE THE MESSAGE as the servant of God when he said that God is like all and God is among all. Then he proclaimed, "None exists but God." God constitutes the whole being, individually and collectively. Every Soul has the divine message within itself, not necessarily within the personality, mind or emotions, but within the Self, which is the same essence that Christians refer to as the Christ. The essence is the same, whatever tradition the words reflect.

"There is no God but God" is again the message in this time. That was and will always be the message. There is no other. You can be awakened to that realization when someone else speaks to you from the God-center, because that essence reaches in and stirs the same essence within you.

In this time, once again, the spiritual message of our oneness with God is being shared, and there is another gift being given as well. The message has been that in the latter days, God would pour His Spirit out upon humanity and would make the heart that was hard become tender and loving. That is the message now, for this time.

JOHN-ROGER

ONE ERA OF CONSCIOUSNESS is being brought to a close, and we are unlocking and flinging open the doors to a new era. The opportunity to transcend the lower levels and move directly into Soul Consciousness is again being offered to those Souls who can recognize it.[1]

---

[1] Soul Transcendence is the work being done through the Movement of Spiritual Inner Awareness. For further information, contact MSIA at P.O. Box 513935, Los Angeles, CA 90051, (323)737-4055, www.msia.org.

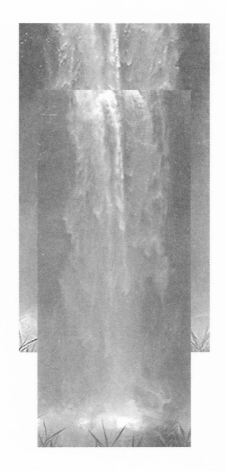

2

DIVINE ESSENCE

JOHN-ROGER

BARAKA...A DIVINE ESSENCE
EXTENDED FROM THE SPIRIT
TO THE HUMAN CONSCIOUSNESS.

PART OF THE SPIRITUAL MESSAGE rests on the frequency of certain words. I use two ancient words at the end of my seminars and Soul Awareness Discourses, "Baruch Bashan," which mean, "the blessings already are." It is a statement that all the blessings that will ever be present exist here and now; all you have to do is move into the realization of those blessings. The frequency of those Hebraic words inherently conveys the blessings to your consciousness.

WITHIN A LINE OF ANCIENT MASTERS of the Sufi tradition, there is a word used mainly in an inner silence to invoke what could be called "virtue from heaven." The word, "Baraka," invokes a special protection and brings a special upliftment. It is not as powerful as the words Baruch Bashan, but it is powerful.

Baraka represents a divine essence extended from Spirit to the human consciousness. Those people who have ascended into the higher realms of Light receive of this essence, bring it forward into this level, and can bestow it upon others.

YOU CAN READ book after book and gain tremendous levels of mental information. Until you can find someone who can bring Baraka to you, however, the information has little value without the experience.

IF YOU RECEIVE BARAKA and let it flow into you, it will flow through every center of your beingness and transform you as it uplifts you. Baraka is an essence of divine energy, divine love.

JOHN-ROGER

THE EXPERIENCE OF BARAKA is described in many ways. It is called the "Holy Spirit," "grace," "seeing the Light," and "hearing the Sound." Baraka is a universal experience.

THE SYMBOLOGY of the word Baraka is interesting. It means taking from above and giving to above, taking from below and giving to above, taking from above and giving to below, and taking from below and giving to below. So as you receive, you give; as you give, you receive. Both actions exist simultaneously in a constant flow.

SOME PEOPLE ARE BUSY just receiving. If this is what
you do, the Baraka within you goes stale and stagnant.
It is much like a river or stream flowing into a lake
from which there is no outlet: the lake becomes
brackish and dead. But if the stream flows into that
which is continuously giving outward, then it always
remains fresh and alive. When you do good works,
Spirit continually delivers Baraka to you. When you
feel you've "got it," "reached it," or "don't need it any
more," it will no longer be delivered to you. Then
you will either have to manufacture it (which is
difficult) or make it up (which is deceitful).

DIVINE ESSENCE

I DON'T LIKE TO SPEAK of spiritual deceit, but there are people who will try to deceive you regarding spiritual issues. There are methods to test the Spirit so that you won't be pulled into areas of deceit. Use them to test what I tell you. If you don't find an attunement ringing with you, then maybe this is not for you. You can find out pretty quickly if these spiritual teachings are something within which you can work and live.

THE WAY TO TEST SPIRIT is very simple. Wherever you go, ask for God's Light to surround you, protect you and fill you. Place it ahead of you wherever you are going so that you will always be well received. Every time you meet someone, ask this Light to be placed between you, not as a barrier, but for clarity. Ask for the highest good to be present.

When people speak to you, ask yourself, "Is this true for me?" You can't ask if it's true for everyone because there is no real truth for everyone—except God. Once you have found God, you have indeed found the universal truth.

WHEN YOU HEAR INFORMATION being presented to you, place the Light between you and the speaker, as a channel for clear communication. Close your eyes for just a second and ask, "If the information I am hearing is not true for me, I would like to be shown this in a clear way. And if this information is right for me, I would like to experience the presence of the Light and Spirit within me in an uplifting way." You will get feedback from Spirit if you ask for clarification in this way. You may feel goose bumps, warmth, or a chill around the top of your head. You may feel a lift in energy. You may feel a sensation or pulsation in your forehead. There are many ways that Spirit might signal you of its presence. If the situation is not right for you, you may get very restless and feel compelled to leave, or get sleepy and drift off for a few minutes. You will have your answer, and you will know it. This is one way to decide the validity—for you—of what you hear.

KEEP IN MIND that what may be valid for one person may not be valid for another. There's truth in the old saying that "one man's medicine is another man's poison." We all must participate in life according to where we come from and where we are going, according to our own life destinies. You can't ask for the truth for a group; you can only ask for truth for yourself. You have a right to ask for the truth for yourself; you don't have the right to inflict your truth or preferences on others.

SOME PEOPLE FAITHFULLY BELIEVE everything they hear or read. That's not the most beneficial way to run your life. That's not practical spirituality. When you hear any information, go home and contemplate it. See if there is a logic in it that works for you. Then see how or if it can work in your life.

YOU MIGHT SAY, "I have a feeling this information wasn't meant for me because it doesn't apply to any of my situations." That may be a valid point of view for now. In a week, however, someone may come to you and say, "I have this problem and don't know how to handle it." You'll remember the information that "wasn't for you," and share it with them. The other person may thank you and tell you that's exactly what they needed to hear.

We call these experiences the "miracles" of working with the Light. You allow the Light to flow through you to others. Information that might not do anything for you in a given moment may be appropriate for someone else in the future, allowing you to be of service and assistance. The Baraka you receive is then extended out to someone else, and the flow is continued.

THERE ARE MANY PARTS to the work that can be done with you through the spiritual master. Strangely enough, one part of that work is to teach you to more effectively handle this physical level, describing and demonstrating techniques to help you overcome the traps of the mind, emotions, and body.

A greater part of the work is to extend Baraka to you, giving you the energy, force, and strength to overcome negativity and lift your consciousness into the positive.

And an even greater part is to work with you to establish you in Soul consciousness, in the realms of pure Spirit, freeing you from recycling endlessly in the lower levels. The greatest joy you will ever experience is when you develop the ability to consciously transcend this physical form through Soul transcendence.

Mental knowledge of these higher realms is not enough. You can "know" a lot of information without really knowing it. You can read what someone else has experienced and "know" it on an intellectual level, but until you have had the experience, the process is like that of a child who sees a flashlight beam on a wall and goes to the wall to get the light. That beam is only a reflection of the light, not its source. Yet many people do a similar thing, going out into the world to see who will reflect Light back to them. They are searching for a form of Light, but aren't going to the source to find it.

You can continually fool yourself by gratifying your own illusion, which causes pessimism and doubt. Then you miss the Baraka that is being continually extended to you. You gain confidence when you use your experience as your teacher.

THERE IS A KIND OF KNOWING that doesn't necessarily come through experience, but through the inner conviction that just knows. Those of you who are men know you are men, and those of you who are women know you are women. You don't need verification from any source outside of yourself to know this. You are what you are. That type of self-evident knowing sometimes appears inside of you when you are presented with spiritual teachings. You know the truth of them.

EVERYTHING BEING BROUGHT TO YOU is Baraka; it is up to you to make all things Baruch Bashan. It is not up to anyone else to change your attitude toward these things; that is something you must change if you choose to. That is your responsibility.

THE SPIRITUAL MASTERS of Light and Sound can extend to you a love that no one else can give you, a love that will not possess you or allow anything to harm you; this is also Baraka. This ancient Sufi word defies description and goes beyond vocabulary. It is the pure essence of Spirit. It is the Source, not the reflection.

The spiritual form represented by a spiritual master gets its power from the Source. It is an agent of the Supreme God. It is not reflection, though the physical body of the master is a reflection.

WHEN YOU SEE A SPIRITUAL MASTER or read or listen to their words, you are experiencing reflections of the consciousness of Baraka, the Baruch Bashan. This essence resides perfectly protected within each individual Soul. The physical manifestations are a mirror image of the greater spiritual reality, and may be distorted, yet they are still part of the spiritual expression.

A SPIRITUAL MASTER is in contact with both the world and the Spirit simultaneously. Most people are like apples that have fallen from the tree (the Source) onto the ground. The spiritual master is like an apple still connected to the tree, on a branch that has bent over and touched all the way to the ground. The apple is both on the ground with the other apples and still connected to the tree.

THE SILENT ONES, who are spiritual forces issuing forth out of God, the Lord of the positive realms of Spirit, work directly in line with the energy of the Mystical Travelers. They are very difficult to find and identify for the simple reason that they are silent. To find them, you must be silent, also.

People have asked me how often I am in contact with the Silent Ones and I answer, "How often are you in contact with your eyes?" All the time. But when you look at something, do you see it or does your mind wander away from it so that you aren't seeing?

Contact with the Silent Ones is a similar process. When you focus there, you find that you've never really left that greater consciousness.

THE WORK THAT GOES ON in this physical world can pull attention away from the Spirit. Asking questions of the Spirit like, "Should I get another job, move to another city, and seek other friends?" doesn't ultimately tend to lift you into a higher consciousness.

Spirit's work with you is much easier when you handle the "ten percent" level of this world as effectively as you can from your present level of knowledge and ability. You can't have 100 percent certainty regarding anything in this world, because you only have ten percent of your total awareness here. Do the best you can with that ten percent; work as close to 100 percent of your ten percent as possible.

PEOPLE WHO WORK to the full capacity of their ten percent have been called geniuses—or sometimes eccentrics—because they are true to their own consciousness and not to the opinions of the world. When you are true to yourself, you learn to maintain the dignity of your own divine consciousness. Then, no matter what your family, employers, friends, or anyone else asks of you, you can respond joyfully as an expression and manifestation of Baraka. You can bypass concerns of "what other people might say or think" and move into doing.

IF YOU DON'T HAVE AN ATTUNEMENT with Spirit, you won't find yourself experiencing Baraka, no matter how much your mind says you are. If you have an attunement with Spirit, then anything you do, no matter how big or small, can be a vehicle for sharing divine love with others. You might find yourself tying a child's shoelaces, cleaning out a friend's garage, giving up your Saturday at the beach to help someone, doing your spiritual exercises[2], sending the Light to those who need your love and support, or any number of other things.

---

[2] Spiritual exercises are an active form of meditation. For more information, see John-Roger's book, *Inner Worlds of Meditation*.

ONCE WHEN I was getting off a plane, I noticed a
very petite woman struggling to get her luggage
from the overhead bin. I could have just kept going
like the other people, but it was a chance to share
Baraka. I got her suitcase down for her and waited
until she could collect her things and step out into
the aisle. She started glowing; the irritation that could
have blocked her left and she was clear. An
acquaintance of mine who was on the same plane
saw this; she thought it was wonderful that I would
help this woman with her luggage, wait for her to go
ahead of me, and go much slower in order to assist
her. But the sharing of Baraka was my pleasure.

ALL THAT SPIRIT ASKS is that you unfold into greater spiritual consciousness and share your awakening with other people. And Spirit will do whatever can be done to assist you in that process of transcendence. That does not necessarily mean that difficult things will be taken from you; it may mean that you are given all the love and support you need to handle your challenges. That help may come to you through others as the divine essence flows through them to you.

TOO OFTEN people want to be the "teacher" to those around them, to be the "great spiritual savior" and lead the next mass exodus to Venus. That's fine if you want to stay in these lower worlds. If you're going to lead the next mass exodus into the spiritual realms, however, you'd better first learn how to drive the bus, punch and collect the tickets, travel the correct routes, and keep your group together, because there are more Souls on the other realms of Light than there are here in this world. There is nothing to fear, but if you don't know your way, you can find yourself at a loss.

MAKE SURE THAT YOU don't overstep your spiritual ability through your words and personality. Be honest with yourself and others. If you have a little knowledge, let people know what your limits are. You can probably assist people by simply being who you are. If they know what to expect, they will learn and grow from what you can share with them and bless you for it. But if you create a false impression of being more than you are, you will fall short of their expectations, and they may curse you for it.

THE POWER OF SPIRIT promotes and perpetuates total honesty in your consciousness. It is no respecter of your dishonesty.

Be honest with yourself and others. It's an important key to your success. When you are freely sharing who you are, you allow divine essence to flow through you to them, and everyone participates in the blessings.

SOME PEOPLE DON'T KNOW how to talk with other people about these ideas of Soul transcendence and Spirit. You can share information with people as you understand it, without judging them by trying to determine beforehand what they can or cannot understand. When you talk to people, you can say, "I don't know how much of this you want to hear. When you've heard enough, just tell me and I'll stop." That's easy. You don't even have to talk about the Light to share it with them, however. Baraka can be shared silently.

ONCE MY STAFF AND I were traveling on a plane when a man sat down beside one of my staff, who turned and said, "Hi." It wasn't fifteen minutes before this man was telling us all the things he had experienced in his travels around the world. We just sat there and listened. Listening to him and enjoying his trip vicariously was a way to share Baraka with him.

He was a perceptive seventy-one-year-old young man, and he started asking some deep questions: "What are you doing? What is this Movement you're part of? How does it work? What does it do? What is your purpose?" When he was finished with his questions, the conversation shifted to other things. That's one way to know when people have received the information they are searching for. A few minutes later this man asked, "May I have one of your business cards? I have a sister, and I think this is what she's been looking for." You might wonder, "What about him? Didn't he want this for himself?" Does it really matter? This man knew what was going on. He had already made the contact and received Baraka.

AT ONE POINT, one of my staff who was twenty-two at the time said to him, "Part of our philosophy is that you can go through life either laughing or crying, but you're going to go through it anyway." The man said, "I'm seventy-one years old, but I never looked at life the way you do; that's a good way to look at it. In fact that makes life much more enjoyable and much more fulfilling."

YOU MIGHT SEE something awkward about a twenty-two-year-old man instructing a seventy-one-year-old man. This gentleman was younger in terms of his openness than he was in terms of his body. He wasn't "old" in the usual sense; he was alive and open. It was wonderful to share Baraka with him and so joyful when he began to share it back with us. We were sharing Light, Spirit, and the love of the Soul. As the sharing continued, other people came closer to be part of it. When the flight was over, we were no longer strangers to each other; we certainly didn't know the details of each other's lives, but we did know each other. And that can be a blessing in this world.

THAT NIGHT THE MYSTICAL TRAVELER took this man into the inner realms and showed him many patterns. He accepted the Spirit; he knew what it was. He's not formally a member of any organization, but he carries information and the spiritual energy to other people.

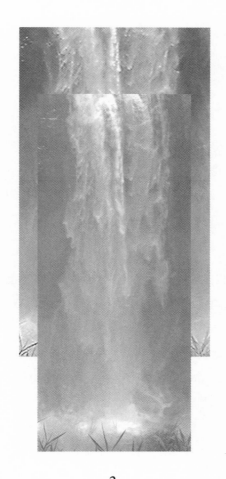

3

THE GAZE OF GOD: TWAJI

JOHN-ROGER

TWAJI IS LIKE THE LIVING WATERS.
YOU ARE WASHED CLEAN, AND IN THAT NEW PURITY,
YOU ACTUALLY START HEARING THE SOUND OF GOD
AS THE SOUND CURRENT FLOODS THROUGH YOU.
IT IS SOMETHING YOU CAN NEVER FORGET.

PART OF SHARING BARAKA with one another involves the communication and connection that is transmitted through the eyes. You know the upliftment you experience when someone who loves you and whom you love looks at you and through their glance conveys all the love they have for you. You see reflected to you your potential, your value and your worth. You see a positive vision of yourself that can sustain you and give you the courage and confidence to grow and expand and express more than you've ever dared before.

THE POWER OF THE GAZE is tremendous. When that is coupled with the energy of pure Spirit, it can shake loose levels of your consciousness that have been covered in layers of deception, tradition, convention, fear, rigidity, and other false images.

I USED TO CONDUCT SEMINARS that began with
people saying their name and sharing something
about themselves with the group. People used to prepare
their sharings days in advance, rehearsing just what
they would say to sound good. When it was their
turn to share, I'd look at them and say, "OK, next," and
they would often say something entirely different than
what they had planned. They spoke spontaneously,
straight from their hearts. People often ended their
sharing by saying something like, "I don't know why
I told you that. I wasn't going to say anything about
that, but now I'm glad I did."

THE POWER OF THE GAZE, when used with the
Traveler Consciousness, is referred to as the "Twaji,"
an Arabic word meaning "the gaze of God." When
that energy is placed toward you, the sincerity of
your beingness surfaces, and in spite of any attempt
to be deceitful, you hear yourself speaking truth and
saying things that are real and present for you. Once
you speak the truth, you clear the deceit from within
you and the energy of Spirit anchors with you. Then
you can transmit Twaji to others. You may talk to a
friend who begins to tell you one thing, but suddenly
tells you something entirely different. They may say,
"I wasn't going to talk about that, but for some reason,
I felt it was important to tell you." The gaze of the
Traveler has gone through you to the next person.
And it will go to the next one and the next and the
next. It's a beautiful way to serve Spirit, as it puts people
in touch with the truth of their own being.

The Gaze of God: Twaji

TWAJI DIFFERS SOMEWHAT from Darshan, which is the vision of the Light that can bring about a form of spiritual enlightenment. Twaji, the gaze of God presented to you through the Traveler consciousness, can go beyond that in its effect. It can establish you in Soul consciousness immediately. This level of the Twaji is often given when a person is getting ready to die. Twaji is presented, and the person immediately transcends the physical and is established in Spirit.

THERE ARE MANY LEVELS to the energy of Twaji. It can be given in a very powerful and direct way or in the most off-handed way. When you think it's going to happen, it usually doesn't. It happens when it happens; it is nothing you can control or manipulate into being. It rarely happens in a group, although it can. You may be sitting in a group with a Master and when they look at you, you experience something flooding through you. Then he looks away and continues with casual conversation because you've received as much of the energy as you can handle.

When you are in the presence of a Master, and can relax and move into a position of acceptance inside of yourself, you are opening yourelf to receive Twaji. If you are defending your point of view, being clever or a "know-it-all," you can block Twaji from coming forward. The energy of Spirit will not inflict on you. It is important to relax and allow things to flow. You can receive much more when you don't seek to restrict yourself or anyone else, on any level.

THE GAZE OF GOD: TWAJI

I OBSERVED ANOTHER SPIRITUAL TEACHER give Twaji within a group situation where it was done so fast that the person receiving Twaji blanked out for a second. It's not unusual for the one receiving Twaji to blank out for a brief moment, leaving the space open for them to be filled anew with living life. Twaji is like the living waters. You are washed clean, and in that new purity, you actually start hearing the Sound of God as the Sound Current floods through you. It is something you can never forget.

THOSE WHO ARE INITIATED into the Sound Current of God often experience Twaji during their spiritual exercises. When you see the eyes of the Traveler appear to you inwardly, you are receiving the Twaji inwardly. In that moment, there is no physical form present to corrupt the Spirit, and you enter into freedom.

As you experience Twaji, you awaken to the Spirit within you, and you move into a new level of responsibility to Spirit. As part of the new responsibility, you must maintain the awareness of Spirit and turn from the negativity of the lower worlds. You must turn away from your hurt, your lust, your greed, and your gossiping. You do this by shifting your attitude.

FOR EXAMPLE, think of someone who was disturbing to you in your childhood. A teacher? A classmate? A friend? Now place yourself into the presence of God's Light and ask yourself how important that person is in your present life, right now. Did the disturbance start quickly leaving you? The Twaji, the Baraka, can come between you and that incident and wash it clean. When you look at anything through the Light of God's Spirit, the positive form is the only thing that will hold steady; you can't hold the negative form. In the moment of letting go of old disturbances, you may even see how they served you and helped you grow. That's the positive form.

JESUS MET A SAMARIAN WOMAN at the well, and He asked her some questions. She tried to put Him off and not answer directly. He turned His countenance upon her and she said to Him, "I know that Messiah cometh, which is called Christ: when He is come, He will tell us all things." Jesus saith unto her, "I that speak unto thee am He." (John 4:25-26) He revealed His ultimate message first to a woman who had had five husbands and was living with a sixth man. He gave the celestial message to a woman. Maybe Jesus really started women's liberation because, prior to that time, women had been used for childbearing and all sorts of labor, but were not considered worthy to receive the message of the Christ, the Messiah, the Light of the world.

SHE NOT ONLY HEARD the words of His message, but by His look, the Twaji, she was transformed and made new. She went and told the men of the village, " 'Come, see a man, who told me all things that ever I did: is not this the Christ?' Then they went out of the city and came unto Him." (John 4:29-30) The gaze of the Master went through her to them, and they all came to Jesus to receive.

DO YOU SEE your responsibility as a Light bearer? You can't put out negativity because you have it wrapped in spiritual energy, and within that is the ability to transform the beingness of another individual. That ability is nothing you can ask for; if the Master gives it to you, you are able to hold it. If it isn't given to you, there is no need to ask. These things are part of spiritual knowledge. You are learning parts now; you may soon know the totality of Spirit as it presents itself to you.

AS YOU GAIN THE DISCIPLINE to express yourself consistently in honest, forthright ways, you are training yourself to hold the vision of Spirit steady within you. As you do your spiritual exercises or meditation, you bring yourself into alignment with the Spirit. As you conduct yourself in ways that are responsible to yourself and not inflictive to others, you bring yourself into line with spiritual guidance. Then you can receive the gifts of Spirit. You prepare yourself to have the gaze of God start working in and through you. If you attempt to get the gifts to abuse or take undue advantage of someone else, you will find yourself blocked and frustrated at every turn. If you only wish to serve God, the gifts you can be given are many.

BE STEADY in your consciousness. As soon as you say, "I'll do this ... no, I'd rather do this ... no, I think I'll do that..." you have split your consciousness. How can you correct the situation? Sit still until your consciousness brings itself together and you see clearly what direction you should take. Do meditation, contemplation, or spiritual exercises as a daily practice. Learn the discipline of consciousness. Hold your gaze steady on your goal. If you are distracted by everything that comes along, you will not reach your goal. Spirit needs those who will move steadily forward.

IN THE LATTER DAYS, there will be many who say, "I am the Light, the Truth and the Way." How will you know the one who speaks truly to you? You will know them by their works. If you have disciplined yourself to complete what you have begun, to treat every person honestly, fairly, and with a loving heart, you will recognize those qualities in others. If you are scattered and inconsistent in your consciousness, your attention will slip, and you won't be able to hold steady long enough to recognize the inconsistencies in others. If you know the discipline of steadiness, you will be able to clearly see when someone else is slipping, and you will not be deceived.

THE GAZE OF GOD: TWAJI

YOU WILL BE KNOWN by what you do. You prepare and you eat your own feast. If you delay because you don't recognize your own worthiness, then there is no need to seek outside of yourself. If you can't find Spirit within yourself, you won't find it anywhere else. Until you give yourself awareness of your own beingness, until you are loyal to your own Soul, until you use the Twaji to gaze inwardly, letting it light the path to your own reality, you will not know God.

THE MYSTICAL CONSCIOUSNESS teaches finding the inner Kingdom, the inner realms of consciousness, the absoluteness and purity of each individual in Soul. Learn those lessons well.

EXPERIENCE YOUR OWN DIVINITY. Receive the Baraka, the Darshan, the Twaji, and use those qualities to grow in your spiritual knowledge and love. Then you will be able to share those qualities with others.

WHEN YOU SEE OTHERS, look into their hearts, not to analyze them, but to find where you can touch them with your love.

WHEN YOU GIVE LOVE, don't hold onto the other end. Give it and let it go completely. The other person is free to do with it as they wish. They can share that love with anyone or with no one. When you give your love and let it go, it doesn't matter to you what they do with it.

DON'T LET ANYONE buy your allegiance. Give your allegiance freely where you want to give it, but don't demand anything in return. If you do, you've sold yourself short, and will no longer be free.

SPIRIT IS GIVEN TO YOU FREELY, and you must receive it freely. There is no other way to receive it. You can't receive Spirit intellectually, emotionally, or physically. You cannot think about it, feel it or touch it. Yet it is more valuable to you than your next breath. It is the living water of life. It is the ocean of divine love and mercy. It is the essence of life itself.

IN SPIRIT, there is no time and no space. Everything exists right now, in eternity, as One. There is no division, no separation. One Soul is all Souls. Jesus said, "He that hath seen me hath seen the Father." (John 14:9) He demonstrated tremendous understanding, seeing Himself through all others.

When you realize that you are all things, you also include yourself. The realizations don't come with mentalizing or talking; they come from the intelligence of the Soul, from the knowledge inherent within you. Gain the knowledge and the understanding of your Self, and you will be able to live your life from a position of wisdom.

IF YOU WANT TO SEE CLEARLY, practice the admonitions of the Buddha, of Jesus the Christ, or of any of the great masters. Practice until they are perfect. In perfection, you will be in your Soul because all of these paths eventually lead to the Soul. If you study religion, do it perfectly. If you study metaphysics, do it perfectly. If you study the science of mind, do it perfectly. It will point the way to your next step of fulfillment and completion.

As you see the Light, you will experience the Twaji. You will see the Light coming out of your own countenance, your own beingness, and then all you do is follow the Light. Remember to follow the Source of the Light, not the reflection. Remember that the Source is in you.

AFTER YOU'VE COMPLETED the pathway you're on, and you see no more Light ahead of you, stop and go within. Recharge the battery. Worship your own beingness, not in selfish love, but in love of the Spirit within you. Give up the lower levels and adore, worship, and love the God essence inside of you. Everything else is reflective and illusory. Spiritual exercises and meditation will point you back to the stability of the spiritual life.

WHEN YOU THINK YOU HAVE to have something in this world, stop and ask yourself, "How do I look through the eyes of God to see if that is good for me?" The gaze of God will start appearing within you. The way will appear before you. The Light will go ahead of you, and you will know your direction.

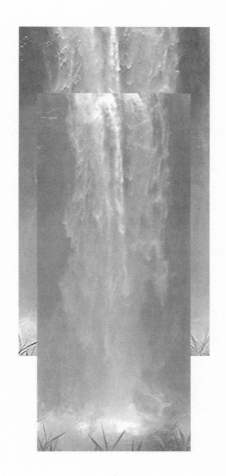

4

LIVING DIVINE ESSENCE

AWAKENING TO THE SOUL
IS NOT AN INTELLECTUAL PROCESS;
IT'S A STATE OF BEING AND DOING.

WHEN YOU BECOME INVOLVED in spiritual teachings coming from the high, positive realms of God-awareness and you open yourself to that transcendent consciousness we call the Mystical Traveler, Spirit often comes forward by means of what orthodox religions call "grace." Jesus said it this way: "For where two or three are gathered together in my name, there I am in the midst of them." (Matthew 18:20) The people Jesus spoke to might not have understood the Sufi word Baraka, so he said it another way, but the meaning is the same. In India, the quality of spiritual blessing is also referred to as Darshan. It is a quality very similar to Baraka transmitted through the eyes from one to another. This essence can be called many names. We know it as divine love, and through divine love we share Baraka with each and every one we meet.

WHEN YOU, in your individual way, tune into divine love, the center where you know goodness dwells, the place where you truly live and express calmly, peacefully and with love, then your behavior becomes a true representation of the Christ within you. When this process starts, you are opening the portals of your Soul. Awakening to the Soul is not an intellectual process; it's a state of being and doing.

As YOUR EXPRESSION becomes more closely matched with the inner integrity of your being, you find yourself moving into the Christ of your inner consciousness. It's a place that has no description, although it may be the greatest level of reality you have ever known. Moving into that reality is like paying your Self a visit. It's like coming home inside of yourself. The joy, bliss and ecstasy that can come forward from that small visit with your Self can carry you through some very rough spots in your life.

SINCE YOU DWELL primarily in negative existence—on a negative planet, in the negative realms of Light, in a negative body—you find a greater number of negative things to work through. And you find the Lord of negative creation, the Kal power, is present to test you and prove to you that you are becoming worthwhile by surviving the snares and pitfalls of the lower realms.

YOU MAY BE REALIZING that reaching the inner consciousness and become aware of your Soul, the divine essence within you, by yourself would probably take a long time. Someone who knows the way can speed up the process. When you work with the Mystical consciousness that can guide you and assist you on this level and all the higher levels, you allow Spirit to work with you more intensely. Spirit is like a fresh breeze blowing from Heaven, making all things new and moving you through all the situations of your life in a spirit of love, friendliness, and acceptance.

WHEN SITUATIONS IN YOUR LIFE become difficult or painful, you may lose track of the fact that Spirit is still present in your life. The situation you perceive as negative may be Spirit's blessing, giving you the opportunity to clear conditions that are holding you back and allowing you to move into greater strength and freedom.

People sometimes ask their spiritual teacher if they will intercede. There are things that are possible, but not allowed. The Holy Spirit rarely comes in and overpowers the negative force or enforces itself in opposition to the negative power, knowing that the negative force is here to perform a job. It is here to test and strengthen you, to prove to you your own worth. When you do not pass a test of negativity, that fact does not make the test an evil or bad process; it's a process that lets you know you still have work to do in that area.

JOHN-ROGER

THE SPIRITUAL MASTER can bring Baraka to your consciousness to assist you in finding the strength and integrity to deal with the situations in your life. They can help awaken you to your own God center so you gain a clear perspective of God's presence in your life and your part in the divine plan.

When you turn to the Light and Love within you, you may discover your connection with the Mystical consciousness. At that point, you may be choosing to break the incarnation pattern with which you have been involved. As you move to break the hold of the lower worlds, you may find the forces of negativity "attacking" you in much more specific ways than before. If you are involved in the conscious and direct pursuit of spiritual transcendence, the negative forces must do their job.

As YOU MEET the challenges that come to you, you are learning the lessons necessary for your growth and upliftment. If you hold strong in your purpose, you will experience, even in the midst of the "attack," the perfect spiritual protection which is extended to you through the consciousness of the Mystical Traveler.

HAVE YOU EVER NOTICED that negativity strikes primarily in the area of your weakness? It rarely tests you in the field of your strength because in that type of showdown, it will lose. The negative forces have a kind of intelligence that will instinctively go for your weak areas. Just about the time you think you've really got an area mastered, the negative power comes in to make sure you've mastered it. If you have, you're free. If you haven't, you find yourself still bound by the laws of the lower worlds. Even when you pass the tests and prove your spiritual strength, you have to continually exercise those strengths in order to maintain them.

YOU'RE NEVER GIVEN anything you can't handle. That's a spiritual law. There may be things that are difficult to handle, that you'd prefer not to handle, or that you'd like to handle better, but everything you are given is within your ability to handle.

WHEN YOU ARE WORKING with the Mystical Traveler, you come under the spiritual protection of the Holy Spirit. The line of the spiritual hierarchy extends through the divine school of the Holy of Holies to the Silent Ones of God. The spiritual connection to the Supreme God is very specific and direct, and the teachings are vital and alive, now. That is why the teachings come alive in our hearts. They are much more than words on a page.

W<small>HEN YOU ARE WORKING</small> with the Mystical consciousness, the work is more inner than outer. You are given teachings inwardly in the purity of your heart and Soul. The outer words, the books and discourses, are reflections of the inner teachings. These outer reflections are only the beginning, not the end; they serve to awaken you to the inner teachings that are going on within you twenty-four hours a day.

The teachings show you how to live in a rightful, upright way, bypassing levels of deceit, lies, cheating and dishonesty. You don't have to express those negative areas unless you want to remain here in the physical world. If you want to remain here on this negative level, all you have to do is give allegiance to lust, anger, avarice, hatred, despair, envy, vanity, and attachment. You guarantee yourself continued life in the negative worlds through these expressions.

IF YOU PREFER TO WALK FREE of the lower worlds and establish yourself in the Spirit, there are only a few qualities that are necessary.

The first one is acceptance. You have to accept what is so in your life and be honest with it, not pretending it's something it's not or creating fantasies about how you would like it to be. Just accept what is.

The second quality is understanding. You have to seek understanding by understanding yourself. You don't necessarily have to understand everyone else, but it's important to know and understand yourself.

The third quality is responsibility. You have to take responsibility for yourself and your actions on all levels.

And the fourth quality is cooperation. Once you accept what is, understand it, and take responsibility for yourself and your actions, you can start cooperating with all of that. When you cooperate, you discover you're free.

IT CAN BE AMAZING to discover that the good Lord did not put you here on earth to be a beggar. He put you here and said, "This is the way to learn about Me..." and showed you a lot of different ways to learn. You can learn through prayer, through loving your family and children, through caring for others, through meditation, through serving others in their time of need, through contemplation, and through many other ways.

As you learn about God, those things that were mysteries to you become clearer. Because there is nothing that is not God, as you begin to know God, you know all things. All becomes One.

WHAT IF THE APPEARANCE of the Messiah begins with you awakening to the God essence inside of you? What if it is discovering that the glory of God resides within you, as well as within all others?

Traditionally, churches have taught that the glory belongs to the Father. And that is true, but it's incomplete. The Father does His work in this world through each one of us, as we do good works. If you, in your everyday life, can allow the Father to do the work of Spirit through you, you will find your life becoming simple and joyful. You will be experiencing Baraka as it flows through you into the world. You don't have to control it, make it happen, or make any decisions about it. All you have to do is accept that it is happening.

WHEN YOU ARE IN THE STATE of acceptance, you're moving past attachment and desire. It's so easy to talk about acceptance, but not necessarily easy to demonstrate it in your life. Once you can demonstrate that first spiritual law, you're in the game. Then you can call in the quarterback, who is called selectivity. Along with it comes discernment. You discern what is available to you and choose what will work best for you. You might ask yourself how well you discern what you are bringing to yourself and how well you test the Spirit.

JOHN-ROGER

ONE OF THE GREAT FOLLIES of following any
particular spiritual path is the temptation to "play
God." You do this by twisting the teachings to say, "I
am spiritual, divine, the essence of God," but forgetting
to ground those ideas into physical reality, which
includes the body, imagination, emotions, mind and
unconscious, with all their inherent illusions.

YOU DON'T HAVE TO PLAY what you are; what you are not, you cannot play. There is no need to misrepresent what is going on. You are not God in the sense of the Supreme God. You do carry within you an essence of God, an essence of the Christ consciousness. Outwardly, you are a reflection of the Soul that is in direct contact with God.

BE CAREFUL NOT TO INFLICT what you identify as your spirituality on other people. Live in simplicity. Live in the truth of your own beingness, and let your actions speak for you.

Until you have the experience of the inner consciousness and spiritual worlds, what I tell you is nonsense—it makes no sense. And when you have had the experience of transcendental consciousness, you are awakened to a different reality and you know its truth. Then there is nothing you have to believe, and you don't have to go on faith. If this sounds like a fairy tale, accept a challenge from me: prove me wrong.

WHEN YOU BEGIN TO AWAKEN to the Soul, you grow spiritually. As you awaken and begin to see yourself in spiritual reality, you'll see the many times you have misrepresented, betrayed and confused yourself. You may be tempted to berate yourself and say, "Look how stupid I've been, I can't be worthwhile." If you can truly open up and allow yourself to perceive yourself clearly, without distortion, you'll see yourself as the Master sees you. You'll know your own worthiness and beauty, and in that moment you'll experience Baraka and move into great loving for yourself. You'll also experience Darshan, which opens your eyes to spiritual reality. If you're not ready, it won't happen. When you're ready, there will be no way you can stop it.

IF YOU'RE WISE, you won't struggle against what is established on this physical level. You'll work within it as you seek to gain greater attunement with higher levels of consciousness. Once you are connected to the Mystical Traveler consciousness and agreement is made to work together, the work goes on twenty-four hours a day. The Traveler does not leave you, no matter what you do physically. The presence of that force within you is the main value of the teachings. The words can be found in many places and are spoken by many. However, when you connect to the presence of Spirit inside you, the teachings are given to you inwardly and become an aspect of your experience.

IF YOU ALWAYS RUN to some physical body to ask physical questions and get physical answers, you may not learn to tune inwardly and go into the subtle levels of your own consciousness. It is important to reach within you to the source of knowledge and strength and to know for yourself what is right to do. On those higher inner levels, you cannot be deceived.

MANY TIMES YOU WILL be placed in a "predicament" which must be solved. If you reach outside of yourself for an answer, you can sometimes get one that assists you temporarily, but in a while you find yourself right back in the same predicament because you did not go through it as a process of learning. You sought a way out of it through someone or something else. So many times the way out of something is to go through it and gain the greatest awareness available to you.

MOVING INSIDE to your own spiritual inner awareness is not always easy to do by yourself. But then, you didn't put yourself into this life all by yourself, either. You were put here as part of the body of God, an heir to the kingdom of Heaven. Usually when you are born into the physical body, you slip behind a veil of forgetfulness and forget your heritage. Then along comes One who has not forgotten, who sees directly into your inner consciousness, to the beauty you are in your Soul, and tells you what that is. And you will know that it is true. I'm not telling you anything you don't know; it's just that you may not remember it until you hear it stated. Then you have the inner experience that verifies it as truth and reality.

IT'S DIFFICULT to have the inner experience of Spirit if you're running around in the world lying and cheating and getting into all sorts of trouble. Many times you get the inner experience of your own sacredness by sitting down and detaching yourself from the physical world through a form of meditation, contemplation or spiritual exercises.

WHEN YOU DO SPIRITUAL EXERCISES, gather your awareness and focus it where two imaginary lines would meet if you drew one from just above the top of each ear, and the other from the very center of your forehead straight through to the back of the head. That area is called the spiritual eye or the third eye. Focusing here will bring your awareness up out of the lower centers of your body, and you will begin to see more clearly. You begin to see spiritually, rather than in terms of this world.

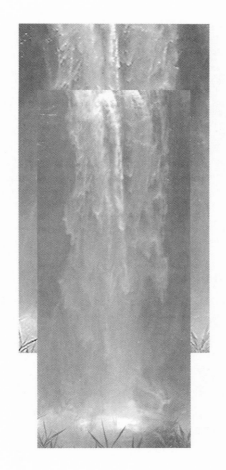

5

AN AGENT OF GOD

JOHN-ROGER

WHEN YOU ARE WATCHING,
BOTH INWARDLY AND OUTWARDLY,
SPIRIT WILL APPEAR TO YOU.

In the beginning was the Word, and the Word was with God, and the Word was God. (John 1:1) And the Word was made flesh and dwelt among us. (John 1: 14) The Word is the energy of God existing in pure Sound. It is the essence. It is the audible Lifestream and Lightstream.

IT IS THROUGH CONNECTION to the Sound Current that you have the opportunity to move back into the heart of God. When you are attuned to the Sound Current, all you have to do is ride the Sound and you will discover its Source, which is God. The Mystical Traveler is an agent for this current of Sound as it issues forth from the Supreme God in the pure realms of Light.

On the lower realms of Light, the Sound and Light are mixed with negative energy. In and above the Soul realm, the Sound Current is pure. It is the most intimately fulfilling melody that sustains you in all things.

PEOPLE HAVE ASKED ME what I do when I am experiencing a "problem" in this world. I move back on the Sound Current into the heart of God where there are no problems, only various aspects of experience. Experiences are a measure of growth, so look forward to your next experience, and you may learn more in your awareness of God.

DO YOU SOMETIMES FIND yourself saying, "I want to experience the awareness of God—why do I have to clean the house or take out the trash?" What do you think God is? Am I trying to tell you that God is a clean house? Perhaps. It's possible. God may be a clean house, a rose, a burning bush, a man, a child, all of these things and much, much more.

WHERE DO YOU GO to find God? Go wherever God is. Since God is everywhere, in everything, entirely and eternally present in your very breath, you can find God by watching and listening. Watch for the Light, both in the physical form and the inner form. Listen for the Sound of God in everything you encounter. When you are watching, both outwardly and inwardly, Spirit will appear to you. It may come to you as Baraka, as the awareness of the blessings in your life. It may come as a peace that transcends all understanding. It may come as the Darshan, as your sight is opened to spiritual reality. However you receive Spirit, in that moment you're going to have a form of transcendental experience.

If you are not quite in attunement with your own divine essence, if you are not having that experience of Baraka, get together with others who seek to know God. Gather together in the name of the Christ, in the consciousness of the Mystical Traveler, in Satsang, or in the consciousness of One. However you identify it, when you are gathering together in God's name, Spirit appears and Baraka is extended to you through the grace of the One God. If you come together and decide to do your own ego trip, however, you weaken the Baraka that would have been extended to you, and you may end up out of balance with your own divine consciousness.

WHEN THOSE WHO CAN manifest Baraka bring it forward into a gathering, the blessings are bestowed instantly on everyone present. If divine essence is brought to you and you don't partake of it and step forward into divine love, you deny the Holy Spirit. To deny this experience is serious on the spiritual levels, but only inasmuch as you block yourself from the reality of your own knowing. Other than that, Spirit doesn't care whether you remain in these lower worlds for two thousand years or one day. If you discover the reality that is, you have completed the lesson of this earthly "classroom" and are able to transcend to another experience.

The ancient law governing bestowal of Baraka states that it must be done by a physical presence. Once the physical presence has bestowed or activated this essence of divine energy, those who have received Baraka can, in turn, bestow it on others. The more you receive of it, the more you can give it to others. This is how you have the authority to do God's work.

It is by your works you are known, not by your words. A lot of people say a lot of things, but are not capable of delivering divine essence, and it's that ability that's important. The reason we meet and come together with a spiritual focus is to open up the channels that can receive of the essence of Spirit. The part of us that receives of Spirit is so vast that we could meet together for a millennium and never be satiated.

No one who has experienced Baraka and maintained a consciousness that is open to the flow of Baraka will feel the negativity of this planet to any great extent. As long as you are open, letting the love flow and directing your Light out, you are receiving and giving of Baraka, the Holy Spirit, the Light and Sound. You are an instrument of Light. The Spirit uses you to bring Light into this physical realm, and it radiates from you to all others on this level. You receive Baraka, and you, in turn, extend Baraka to all you meet. You lift others by your presence and by your Light. No matter what they say or do, no matter what happens, you still function as a channel for the Spirit, to be used or abused; it matters very little either way.

IF YOU ARE ABUSED, the Light handles that. If you are used, the Light handles that. All you have to do is keep freedom in your consciousness and be open to let Light and love flow through you to everything. You don't have to say, "God bless that flower, that ant, those buildings, that tree." The blessings flow automatically, as soon as Spirit uses you as a channel into this world.

IF YOU DO TAKE your consciousness and direct it toward something—a rose bush, for example—loving and blessing it, it will bear more abundantly. If you pray over seeds with your love, saying, "I will plant you, and you will grow and be magnificent," it will stir the life force within the seed and give it the promise to fulfill.

HUMAN BEINGS GROW in awareness in a similar way. God uses us with one another as instruments of Light. Being together in God's name, in the divine love of Spirit, becomes a prayer. You are a walking prayer, even if you say nothing, because Spirit knows your needs. It knows your desires and your wants, too, and will fulfill them according to your awareness. It will not violate your consciousness; it will sustain the energy within you and give you the ability to continually lift into higher and greater awareness.

AN AGENT OF GOD

THOSE OF YOU WHO WORK with the Mystical consciousness are offered the Holy Spirit. Baraka is extended to you. If you recognize what you have, it enhances your Spirit. If you don't recognize it, your Spirit still sleeps. The Light is given to you consciously; it stirs the intellect and the Soul into recollection of what it really is, its promise and destiny. It is up to you to look into your own consciousness and see the Light and love there. You will see the portals and the keys to the Kingdom of Heaven.

THE PATHWAY is being opened for you. The place is being prepared. You're helping to build it. You will know it more completely when your consciousness is strong, dedicated, and devoted. Then you can say, "I don't care what it takes. I'm going to find the Spirit. I'm just going to do it. My depression can be a stepping stone for me. My doubt can be a stepping stone. I don't have to stumble on these things; I can use them to my advantage." When you reach that point in your consciousness, you can begin moving into the higher realms of Spirit.

Don't get caught in thinking that you know everything; when you do that, you deny the truth that is all around you. There is truth everywhere. There is Light everywhere. The Sound of God is everywhere. The master forces working with the Traveler have the keys and techniques to liberate you in your consciousness while you're still in the physical body; there are others who can do that as well.

ONE KEY TO LIBERATION is eternal vigilance. Salvation is a daily job, a nightly job, and an eternal job. If you enter into spiritual discipline and gain a certain level of awareness, you are responsible for that expansion, and you are responsible for continuing it. You can't stop and "rest on your laurels." It doesn't work that way. You keep going.

An Agent of God

We sometimes talk about being on a spiritual path, but that's a misnomer, for there is no path. There is no distance. There is no "end" to this discovery. You are already all that you will be. You are already that which you seek. The blessings already are, and all you need to do is open your eyes and see that. All you need is the realization.

THE KEYS TO REALIZATION are in the Mystical Traveler consciousness—not in the words that are spoken or written, but in the consciousness itself. The verbal or written level is just a part of the ten-percent physical manifestation. Ninety percent of your beingness lives in the invisible levels around and within you. The spiritual levels go on and on. They are infinite and eternal. Because you don't perceive them doesn't mean they aren't present. You don't perceive radio waves until you turn on the radio. In a similar way, you may not be aware of Spirit until you have an instrument to tune into it. You have that instrument—you are that instrument. But you may not have tuned yourself to receive Spirit.

Part of the Traveler's work is to teach you how to attune yourself to the Spiritual energy that is present. One way that is done is to present spiritual energy to you continuously. As you receive that spiritual energy, it awakens the spiritual energy in you. Then the changes happen from the inside out.

GOD IS THE GREATEST LEVEL of reality you can experience. It is pure Light and Sound. It is the Source. It is not an image, reflection or illusion. It is the only reality. That reality exists within you. It is your Soul. You can drop all the illusions, images and facades. You can go inside and find what is real within you. You can discover God dwelling within.

As you move to that awareness, you experience the grace of God in your life. You experience Darshan, the clear sight. You experience the Twaji, the gaze of God that lifts you into the high realms of Soul consciousness. You experience Baraka, the essence of divine love.

An Agent of God

IF YOU ATTEMPT TO RECONCILE in your mind the seeming paradox of God in the flesh and God in the invisible realms, you will falter and fall into your own doubt, confusion, and despair. Some churches call it sin, but it's mostly despair. Grab yourself by the bootstraps. Forgive yourself for the confusions and disturbances you've perpetrated against yourself. Resolve to take your next breath in love. Resolve to breathe in God in your next breath. You're breathing the same air that Jesus the Christ, Buddha, Krishna, Muhammad and all the other great spiritual teachers and leaders of all times breathed. With each breath you can awaken yourself to greater and greater spiritual awareness.

PRACTICE SPIRITUAL EXERCISES. Practice seeing the Light. Practice hearing the Sound. Practice seeing yourself through the eyes of the Master. Practice the Mystical Traveler consciousness.

An Agent of God

You don't have to go very far to be in Heaven; Spirit is nearer than your own hands and feet. You already are what you wish to be. You are already Light. You are already the divine perfection in your Soul. You are already love. You are already peace. There is a place prepared for you in Heaven. Let's go.

NO ONE COMES TO THE TRAVELER who will not be lifted. These, too, can be the words you pray and the consciousness you demonstrate: "No one will come to me that I do not radiate to them something of the greatness of the Spirit, of divine love and Light, of Baraka." You can do this. These things are of greater service to humanity than I can express in words. These things simply are.

The Prayer of the Master

MY PEACE I GIVE TO YOU because I have peace, and my love I give to you because I have love. I give you to you because I am all. I am everlasting, Alpha and Omega. I am the eternal Now, the manna that falls from heaven. I am self-realized and all is here for me, right now, in this moment. And because I am these things, and because you and I are one, you are these things also.

My realization may be greater at this point in time, but that is the only difference between your consciousness and mine. Through Baraka we are one, and all is shared now. We say together, "Father, Mother, God, I am so happy for my knowledge of you. I will use my awareness for Thy glory alone because I am your instrument. Whatever I do, I do in your name. I do all things in God's name, with the inner Master to work with me and guide me."

As you experience and express your divinity, the shackles of negativity fall away, the past dissolves, and you step into those heavenly planes where the great Masters of Light are waiting to welcome you home to that which is your heritage.

JOHN–ROGER

BARUCH BASHAN
THE BLESSINGS ALREADY ARE
THE BLESSINGS ARE ALL READY

GLOSSARY

BARAKA. Sufi word meaning divine energy, divine love extended by Spirit, through its agent, to those doing good works.

BARUCH BASHAN. Hebrew words meaning "the blessings already are." The blessings of Spirit exist in the here and now.

DARSHAN. A vision of the Light, a spiritual blessing, transmitted through the beingness of a spiritual teacher, often through the eyes. Can bring about an immediate elevation of consciousness.

HOLY OF HOLIES (DIVINE SCHOOL OF HOLY OF HOLIES). The immediate energy spot of God and the surroundings that are affected in a special way by God's energy.

KAL OR KAL POWER. The power of the Lord of all the negative realms. Manifests the magnetic Light. Has authority over the physical realm, including the planet, the body, the imagination, the emotions, the mind, and the unconscious. Called "the prover" because has prime directive to distract into illusions of the world, until we are proved worthy to enter the kingdom of heaven. Kal has no power over the Soul, nor over the Christ power who is the spiritual head of the planet, nor over the Mystical Travelers.

LEVELS OF CONSCIOUSNESS. Planes or realms of existence beyond the physical universe, which

correspond to the elements of human consciousness (imagination, mind, emotions, subconscious, unconscious, and Soul). Negative levels of consciousness and corresponding human consciousness tool: astral realm with tool of the imagination; causal realm with tool of emotions; mental realm with tool of mind; etheric realm with tools of subconscious and unconscious. Positive levels of consciousness: Soul realm and above with Soul as vehicle.

LIGHT. The energy of Spirit that pervades all levels of consciousness. The highest spiritual Light has its source in the Soul realm and above, and is also known as the Light of the Holy Spirit. The magnetic light is the Light of God that functions in the negative realms, is not as high as the Light of the Holy Spirit, and does not necessarily function only for the highest good.

MOVEMENT OF SPIRITUAL INNER AWARENESS (MSIA). An organization whose major focus is to conduct the Soul back to God. Teaches Soul Transcendence, which is becoming aware of oneself as a Soul and, more than that, as one with God.

MYSTICAL TRAVELER CONSCIOUSNESS. A spiritual consciousness that exists throughout all levels of God's creation. Resides within each one of us and is a guide into the higher levels of Spirit, the greater reality of God. Can assist a person in clearing karma (balancing past actions); its work is done inwardly, on the spiritual levels. This consciousness is always anchored on the planet through a physical form.

SATSANG. Being in the presence of a spiritual teacher or guide who offers the teachings of Spirit. Communion with Spirit through a spiritual energy. May take place in the presence of such a being or in a gathering to view a video presentation or listen to an audio seminar.

SILENT ONES. Spiritual forces issuing forth out of the Supreme God. God's creator. Amplify, manifest, maintain and stabilize what God spoke.

SOUL. Essence of God in the physical body. Extension of Spirit that is individualized and can be aware of itself. Positive element in human body in a negative level of consciousness.

SOUND. The Sound Current that can be heard during spiritual exercises. To be followed back to the heart of God. Part of the trinity within everyone, the Light and love and Sound.

SOUND CURRENT. The audible energy that flows from God through all realms. The spiritual energy on which a person returns to the heart of God.

SPIRITUAL EXERCISES. Chanting the HU, the Ani-Hu, or one's initiatory tone. An active technique of

bypassing the mind and emotions by chanting a tone to connect to the Sound Current. Assists a person in breaking through the illusions of the lower levels and eventually moving into an awareness of the Soul consciousness and above.

TEN-PERCENT LEVEL. The physical level of existence, as contrasted with the 90 percent of a person's existence that is beyond the physical realm. The 90-percent level is that part of a person's existence beyond the physical level; that is, one's existence on the astral, causal, mental, etheric, and Soul levels.

TWAJI. An Arabic word meaning the gaze of God. Can be experienced during spiritual exercises from the Mystical Traveler or a spiritual master working from the Soul level and above. Effect may be life-changing toward responsibility to Spirit.

BIBLIOGRAPHY

AUDIO AND VIDEO TAPES, AND TAPE ALBUMS

Items are audio tapes unless otherwise noted. "V" preceding a number denotes the tape is also available in video format. SAT stands for Soul Awareness Tapes, which are audio tapes of J-R seminars, meditations, and sharings that are sent each month only to SAT subscribers. Once you subscribe, you can obtain previously issued tapes. Please note that some of the tapes in this Bibliography are SAT tapes, and you would need to subscribe to the series in order to order them.

AUDIO AND VIDEO TAPES

ANI-HU (MUSIC AND MEDITATION), (#1610, PUBLIC TAPE)

APPROACHING GOD THROUGH GRACE, (#7420, SAT TAPE)

ARE YOU DOING GOD'S WILL?, (#7674, SAT TAPE)

ARE YOU THE SPIRITUAL SKY?, (#3008)

AWAKENING TO THE MYSTICAL TRAVELER CONSCIOUSNESS, (#2017)

BARAKA, (#2054)

BASIC INSTRUCTIONS FOR SPIRITUAL EXERCISES, (#7535, SAT tape)

CATHEDRAL OF THE SOUL, (#3714)

CHANGING YOUR BEHAVIOR TO A SPIRITUAL NATURE (NOV. 95), (#7594, SAT TAPE)

CHANTING THE SACRED TONES, (#7001, SPANISH/ENGLISH)

DISCOURSES AND THE VALUE OF INTROSPECTION, (#7234)

THE DIVINE PROCESS, (#2597)

GO TO THE GOD INSIDE, (#7443, SAT TAPE)

GOD IS INTENTION, (#7354, #V-7354)

GOING HOME ON THE INWARD PATH (DEC. 91), (#7438, SAT TAPE)

THE GOLDEN THREAD OF DIVINITY, (#7466, #V-7466)

BIBLIOGRAPHY

GOSPEL OF ST. JOHN: SPIRITUAL HERITAGE OF MAN/THE SPIRITUAL PROMISE, BY JOHN-ROGER, (#7217)

GUIDANCE INTO THE HEART OF GOD (FEB. 71), (#7557, SAT TAPE)

THE HIERARCHY OF CONSCIOUSNESS, (#7114, SAT TAPE)

THE HU MEDITATION, (#1800)

HU-MAN—GOD MAN, (#7328, SAT TAPE)

IMPULSE OF THE SOUL, (#7395, #V-7395)

INITIATION—MOLDING THE GOLDEN CHALICE, (#2601)

INNER JOURNEY THROUGH SPIRIT REALMS, (#7251)

INNERPHASING FOR MULTIDIMENSIONAL CONSCIOUSNESS, (#7694)

INTRODUCTION TO MSIA, (#7023, #V-7023)

KEEP GOD AS YOUR FOCUS (DEC. 90), (#7425, SAT TAPE)

THE LIGHT, THE TRUTH, AND THE WAY, (#7571, ONE OF SEVEN TAPES IN THE "SPIRITUAL HERITAGE" SERIES, PUBLIC TAPE)

LOOK INTO THE DIVINE, (#2598)

THE MAJESTY OF THE INNER MASTER, (#2625)

MANIFESTING THE UNMANIFEST REALITY, (#2589)

THE MYSTICAL PATH IS THE NATURAL PATH, (#2587)

THE MYSTICAL TRAVELER CONSCIOUSNESS, (#1021)

MYSTICAL TRAVELER: DIRECT LINE TO GOD, (#7127, #V-7127)

PASSAGES TO THE REALMS OF SPIRIT, (#7037, #V-7037)

PRACTICAL KEYS TO DOING S.E.'S, (#7193, SAT TAPE)

PSYCHIC VIOLENCE, (#7308, #V-7308)

SOUND CURRENT, (#2021)

SOUNDS OF THE REALMS, (#2530)

BIBLIOGRAPHY

Soul Realm Mock-up and Beyond, (#7459, SAT tape)

Stalking the Spirit, (#7347, #V-7347)

The Spiritual Warrior/El Guerrero Espiritual, (#7333, #V-7333, English/Spanish)

To the God Within, (#7215)

The Traveler—the One who Laughs in Your Heart, (#2602)

Twaji—The Gaze of God, (#2584)

Twelve Approaches to Spirituality, (#2619, SAT tape)

Twelve Signs of the Traveler, (#1362, SAT tape)

Upgrading our Addictions to God, (#7487, SAT tape)

The Value in Surrendering to God Consciousness, (#7595, SAT Tape)

Walking the Straight and Narrow, (#7379, SAT Tape)

What is the Blessing of Soul Transcendence?, (#1131, SAT tape)

What is Divinity?, (#7585, #V-7585)

What is the Value of Soul Transcendence?, (#1131, SAT tape)

When the Mystical Traveler Works with You, (#2053)

Where are the Worlds Without End?, (#V-7125)

We Must Find God Ourselves (Mar. 71), (#7532, SAT Tape)

Worship God with Your Soul (May 86), (#7476, SAT Tape)

Your Inner World: The Last Frontier, (#7260)

Your Spirit, Key to the Gate, (#4019, SAT Tape)

BIBLIOGRAPHY

TAPE ALBUMS

THE ANOINTED ONE, (FIVE-TAPE ALBUM, #3906)

INNER WORLDS OF MEDITATION, WITH JOHN MORTON (SIX-TAPE ALBUM, #3915, OR CD, #CD-3915, PUBLIC TAPE)

LIVING IN GRACE, (SIX-TAPE ALBUM, #3903, PUBLIC TAPE)

SOUL JOURNEY THROUGH SPIRITUAL EXERCISES, (THREE-TAPE ALBUM WITH BOOKLET, #3718)

SPIRITUAL EXERCISES INNERPHASING, (TWO-TAPE ALBUM WITH BOOKLET, #3810)

SPIRITUAL EXERCISES: WALKING WITH THE LORD, (FOUR-TAPE ALBUM WITH BOOKLET, #3907, PUBLIC TAPE)

SPIRITUAL WARRIOR, (THREE-TAPE ALBUM, #3980, PUBLIC TAPE)

THE WAYSHOWER, BY JOHN ROGER, (TWO-TAPE ALBUM WITH BOOKLET, #3901, PUBLIC TAPE)

BOOKS

BOOKS ARE AVAILABLE AT YOUR LOCAL BOOKSTORE OR THROUGH MSIA.

THE CHRIST WITHIN & THE DISCIPLES OF CHRIST WITH THE COSMIC CHRIST CALENDAR, (#935-1)

FORGIVENESS, THE KEY TO THE KINGDOM, (#934-3)

GOD IS YOUR PARTNER, (#927-7)

JOURNEY OF A SOUL, (#967-X)

INNER WORLDS OF MEDITATION, (#977-7)

THE PATH TO MASTERSHIP, (#916-5)

SPIRITUAL WARRIOR: THE ART OF SPIRITUAL LIVING, (#936-X)

THE TAO OF SPIRIT, (#933-5)

WALKING WITH THE LORD, (#930-0)

BIBLIOGRAPHY

SOUL AWARENESS DISCOURSES

The heart of John-Roger's teachings, Soul Awareness Discourses, provide a tool for gaining greater awareness of ourselves and our relationship to the world and to God. Each year's study course includes twelve lessons, one for each month. Discourses offer a wealth of practical keys for more successful living. Even more important, they provide keys to greater spiritual knowledge and awareness of the Soul.

SOUL AWARENESS TAPE (SAT) SERIES

Membership to the SAT series provides a new seminar by John-Roger each month, on a variety of topics ranging from practical living to spiritual upliftment. In addition, the entire SAT library of hundreds of seminars and meditations is available to Sat subscribers.

THE NEW DAY HERALD

A bi-monthly publication which includes articles by John-Roger as well as informative pieces and a calendar of events around the world sponsored by The Movement of Spiritual Inner Awareness and Peace Theological Seminary & College of Philosophy.

A one-year subscription is free upon request.

LOVING EACH DAY

Loving Each Day is a daily e-mail message that contains an uplifting quote or passage from John-Roger or John Morton. These messages are intended to inspire you and give you pause to reflect on the Spirit within. Loving Each Day is available in four languages: English, Spanish, French and Portuguese.

A subscription is free upon request.

To subscribe, please visit the web site—www.msia.org

BIBLIOGRAPHY

MSIA ON THE **INTERNET**

★ www.msia.org

The web site offers a free subscription to MSIA's daily inspirational e-mail, Loving Each Day; the New Day Herald on-line; the opportunity to request that names be placed on the prayer list; MSIA's catalog, and much more.

★ LOVING EACH DAY E-MAIL

Daily inspirational quotes from John-Roger and John Morton sent to your e-mail address. Free subscription is available in English, Spanish, French and Portuguese. Request Loving Each Day from www.msia.org.

★ LIST OF MSIA INTERNET SITES

www.forgive.org

www.lovingeachday.org

www.ndh.org

www.mandevillepress.org

www.msia.org

www.networkofwisdoms.org

www.pts.org

www.religionfreedom.org

www.seeding.org

www.spiritualwarrior.org

www.tithing.org

BIBLIOGRAPHY

Tapes, books and subscriptions are available from MSIA at the address below. We welcome your comments and questions. Please contact us at

MSIA®

P.O. Box 513935

Los Angeles, CA   90051-1935

323-737-4055   FAX 323-737-5680

soul@msia.org

www.msia.org

ABOUT THE AUTHOR

A TEACHER AND LECTURER of international stature, with millions of books in print, John-Roger has helped people to discover the Spirit within themselves and find health, peace, and prosperity for over three decades.

With two co-authored books on the *New York Times* Bestseller List, and more than three dozen books and audio albums, John-Roger is an extraordinary resource on many subjects. He is the founder of the nondenominational Church of the Movement of Spiritual Inner Awareness (MSIA) which focuses on Soul Transcendence; President of the Institute for Individual and World Peace; Chancellor of the University of Santa Monica; and President of Peace Theological Seminary & College of Philosophy.

John-Roger has given over 5,000 seminars worldwide, many of which are televised nationally on his cable program, "That Which Is." He has been a featured guest on the "Roseane Show," "Politically Incorrect," and CNN's "Larry King Live," and appears regularly on radio and television.

An educator and minister by profession, John-Roger continues to transform the lives of many by educating them in the wisdom of the spiritual heart.

If you've enjoyed this book, John-Roger has written many others for your enjoyment and upliftment. The Bibliography lists a number of his books, audio and videotapes, and you can explore a wider selection on the web site: www.msia.org.